What Do You Think?

Should We Ever Negotiate With Terrorists?

John Meany

Heinemann
LIBRARY

www.heinemann.co.uk/library
Visit our website to find out more information about Heinemann Library books.

To order:
 Phone 44 (0) 1865 888112
 Send a fax to 44 (0) 1865 314091
 Visit the Heinemann bookshop at www.heinemann.co.uk/library to browse our catalogue and order online.

First published in Great Britain by Heinemann Library, Halley Court, Jordan Hill, Oxford OX2 8EJ, part of Harcourt Education.

Heinemann is a registered trademark of Harcourt Education Ltd.

Editorial: Andrew Farrow and Rebecca Vickers
Design: Steve Mead and Q2A Solutions
Picture Research: Melissa Allison
Production: Alison Parsons

Originated by Chroma Graphics Pte. Ltd.
Printed and bound in China by Leo Paper Group

ISBN 978 0 431 11014 1 (hardback)
12 11 10 09 08
10 9 8 7 6 5 4 3 2 1

British Library Cataloguing in Publication Data
Meany, John
Should we ever negotiate with terrorists? – (What do you think?)
1. Terrorism – Government policy – Juvenile literature
2. Terrorism – Juvenile literature
I. Title
303.6'25

Acknowledgements
The publishers would like to thank the following for permission to reproduce photographs:

©Corbis pp. **38** (epa/Abukar Albadri), **8** (Reuters/ Dept. of Defense), **16** (Reuters/Kevin Lamarque); ©Getty Images pp. **47** (AFP Photo/Marwan Ibrahim),p. **50** top (Hulton Archive/Keystone/ Stringer); Courtesy of Middle School Public Debate Program p. **19**; ©PA Photos pp. **37**, **15**, **15** bottom (PA Archive), **27**, **43**, **44** (AP Photo), **33** (AP Photo/ Dita Alangkara), **34** (AP Photo/Jordao Henrique), **42** (AP Photo/Luis Ramirez), **22** (AP Photo/Musa Sadulayev), **25** (AP Photo/Nasser Ishtayeh), **28** (AP Photo/Vadim Ghirda), **48** (AP Photo/Muhammed Muheisen); ©Photoshot p. **31** (UPPA/Landov); ©Rex Features p. **10**; ©Superstock p. **4** (Gala); ©The Bridgeman Art Library p. **12** (Musee de la Ville de Paris, Musee du Petit-Palais, France).

Cover photograph: Cover photograph of masked Palestinian Militants of the Al-Aqsa Martyrs Brigade reproduced with permission of SAID KHATIB/AFP/ Getty Images. Frame from ©istockphoto.com

Every effort has been made to contact copyright holders of any material reproduced in this book. Any omissions will be rectified in subsequent printings if notice is given to the publishers.

The publishers would like to thank Luke Howie for his assistance with the preparation of this book.

Disclaimer

Table of Contents

Some words are shown in bold, **like this**. You can find out what they mean by looking in the glossary.

> *Terrorism is universal!*

Terrorists have come from every country, ethnic group, and social class. Some want to overthrow governments. Others seek revenge for wrongs done to family and friends. Poverty, isolation, tradition, and cultural and religious issues may influence a person's decision to become a terrorist.

Should We Ever Negotiate With Terrorists?

It is difficult, if not impossible, to defend or justify an act of terror. Modern terrorism is extremely violent and destructive. It often targets innocent people. There is a broad agreement among international organizations, government officials, human rights activists, religious organizations, and the public that terrorism should be condemned. So, the debate on terrorism always revolves around how to stop it. Some people argue that military force should be used. Some make the point that terrorism is a crime that the police should investigate. Others argue that it is better to bargain or **negotiate** with terrorists. Should governments ever negotiate with terrorists? For some, this seems impossible. People have difficulty imagining their government communicating in any way with their enemies.

If terrorism cannot be defended, how is it possible to debate or argue about it? The British government secretly negotiated with the **paramilitary** organization, the Irish Republican Army (IRA), for years in an attempt to end the violence in Northern Ireland. The United States has negotiated with Libya's leader, whom it held responsible for plane terror bombings that killed hundreds. Were these good decisions? Discussing terrorism does not mean defending terrorists or their actions. It involves working out ways to stop it. This book will help you join in this important debate by giving you the information and skills you need.

Recognizing terrorists

Who is a terrorist? In some cases, such as in the attacks on the United States on 11 September 2001 where over 3,000 people died, it is clear. In other cases, it may be more confusing to decide which person or group is genuinely involved in terrorism. In violent or political conflicts, the enemy is often labelled as "terrorist". Tibetans call the Chinese they see as invaders terrorists—the Chinese reply that Tibetan resistance fighters are terrorists. The Israelis describe Palestinian **Hamas** suicide bombers as terrorists— Palestinians reply that Israeli destruction and bombing in Palestinian territory are "acts of terror". Russians react angrily to terrorist bombings and kidnappings in their country by people from Chechnya. In turn, Chechens claim they are using self-defence against widespread Russian terrorism in their republic.

Governments sometimes struggle against groups who work against them. The Colombian government fights drug dealers, called narco-terrorists. Leaders in Lebanon, Afghanistan, and Pakistan investigate and prosecute extreme Islamic terrorist groups. Rural farmers use armed violence against officials in Peru and Nepal. In each case, the harder one side attacks, the stronger the other side hits back. If self-defence is involved, can the person still be a terrorist? Is there any truth in the idea that one person's freedom fighter is another person's terrorist? Are some people who are identified as terrorists simply acting against violence and oppression?

Sleepers

One of the strategies of terrorist groups is to let their people live "normal" lives in communities until they are called on to commit an act of terror. They are known as "sleepers". Knowledge of the community makes it easier for terrorists to understand how to make a successful attack. It also means that terrorists have the correct identification papers, employment and school records, and other information that makes it easier for them to hide their plans from the officials.

Until terrorists commit acts of violence, they are difficult to identify. The hijackers who flew the planes during the terrorist attacks in the United States on 11 September 2001 included university students, teachers, and community workers. Their careers did not stop them from committing acts of mass violence. The terrorists responsible for the bombings on the London Underground and a bus on 7 July 2005 had not previously been in trouble with the police. Their neighbours, families, and friends had no idea that when they left their homes that day, they planned to carry out an attack that would take their lives and those of more than 50 innocent people.

Defining terrorism

To understand terrorists, and terrorism and its causes, it is important to know what "terrorism" is. Although there are many definitions for terrorism, the one below is the most common.

What is terrorism?

Terrorism is the use of violence or the threat of violence in order to force a population or government to meet demands.
It has three parts:

✔ **a threat of violence**

✔ **a target, usually civilian or innocent**

✔ **a political aim (for example, the overthrow of a government or the release of jailed prisoners).**

Using fear

Terrorists use violence to promote fear. The traditional acts of terrorist groups included kidnapping and assassination of political and community leaders. The violence was often directed at a single individual. More recently, terrorists have used plane hijackings, bombings, and biological weapons to create panic and get publicity for their group or cause. They have attacked airports, train stations, shopping centres, and skyscrapers. In the future, it is more likely that terrorists will attempt to use **weapons of mass destruction** (WMD) to threaten communities, or even countries. These might include chemical, biological, radiological, and nuclear weapons. These powerful weapons could be used to attack a food supply or an entire city. Sophisticated terrorists could use the internet to target businesses or disrupt a country's economy.

Sleepers are waiting

"We know there are sleeper cells [of terrorists] still lurking in this country, plotting to harm us and providing support for future attacks. Some have been arrested, some are under surveillance, and I'm sure some are still at large."

Senator Charles Grassley of Iowa, 9 September 2003

> *The Khobar Towers attack*

Members of Saudi Hezbollah, a group in favour of the closure of U.S. military bases in Saudi Arabia, attacked the Khobar Towers apartments, where many U.S. personnel lived, with a fuel truck bomb in June 1996. Despite a partial evacuation of the buildings and protective blast walls, 20 people were killed and almost 400 wounded in the explosion. The al-Qaeda organization of Osama bin Laden believes the continuing presence of the United States in Saudi Arabia is an insult to Islam and its holy places in that country.

Acts of terror threaten innocent people

There are terrorist organizations that try to avoid the deaths of innocent people. Terrorists have been known to alert the police to evacuate a building before a bombing. They may only attack official government buildings or the armed forces and police. The majority of terror groups, however, try to disrupt everyday life or convince the public that their government cannot protect them. These groups make innocent civilians the targets of violence.

Enemies as terrorists

People who are involved in conflicts frequently describe their enemies as terrorists. If an enemy is a called a "terrorist", the implication is that the enemy is violent, ruthless, and unpredictable. This can help motivate people and groups to support your side in a struggle against terror.

The fact that a person is called a terrorist does not necessarily make that person a terrorist. It is more important to judge terrorism by behaviour. Has a person or group participated in violence? Did the violence target an innocent population? Was it done to support a political leader or cause? Is it likely that other innocent people will be threatened in the future? If the answer to these questions is "yes" it is likely that the person is a terrorist. These excerpts from speeches by U.S. President George Bush and the international al-Qaeda leader Osama bin Laden make this point.

 Describing the "enemy"

"… the name of the American government and the name of Clinton [U.S. President, 1992–2000] *and Bush* [U.S. President, 1988–1992] *directly reflect in our minds the picture of children with their heads cut off before even reaching one year of age…The President has a heart that knows no words…To these mothers I say if they are concerned for their sons, then let them object to the American government's policy and to the American president. Do not let themselves be cheated by his standing before the bodies of the killed soldiers describing the freedom fighters in Saudi Arabia as terrorists. It is he who is a terrorist who pushed their sons into this* [conflict] *for the sake of the Israeli interest."*

– Osama bin Laden, March 1997

"We remember the horror of watching planes fly into the World Trade Center, and seeing the towers collapse before our eyes. We remember the sight of the Pentagon, broken and in flames…We remember the cold brutality of the enemy who inflicted this harm on our country—an enemy whose leader, Osama bin Laden, declared the massacre of nearly 3,000 people that day—I quote—'an unparalleled and magnificent feat of valor, unmatched by any in humankind before them.'"

– President George W. Bush, 6 September 2006

> *Shocked and confused*

Nothing can prepare someone for becoming a victim of a terrorist act. This woman, suffering from burn injuries, is being helped away from the scene of the terrorist attacks in London on 7 July 2005.

The History Of Terrorism

Terrorism can be traced back thousands of years. Kidnapping, assault, and murder of political officials and members of the public are popular terrorist tactics. Throughout history, terrorist organizations have violently resisted governments. They have objected to governments that excluded or outlawed them and kept them out of meaningful political participation. Those who turned to terror may have been denied citizenship, the right to vote or to speak freely, or the ability to practise their religion. They may have been persecuted for their race, nationality, or class. A government might have made an effort to act lawfully and fairly for all its citizens, but a minority objected to that decision. The history of terrorism is the history of political **dissent**, the violent disagreement with government or authority. But it is also the history of criminals, the mentally deranged, and religious, nationalist, and cult fanatics.

As weapons became more destructive and easier to hide, terrorists increasingly used explosives or poisons to target their official enemies or threaten civilians. When military and police targets became more secure it was difficult to attack them. The move to terror attacks on civilian targets could also spread fear. That is why bombings in public places—markets, transport centres, nightclubs, restaurants, hotels, even schools—are now the most common modern terror tactic.

Revolutionary "terror"

The modern history of terrorism, including the word, "terrorism", began at the end of the 18th century. Terror, at that time, was not as negative an idea as it is today. Terrorism was, in fact, a term used positively by the leaders of the French Revolution. The revolution had overthrown the **monarchy** and established French democracy. They organized a Committee of Public Safety to execute anyone who was a threat to the new government. The revolution's leader at the time, Maximilien Robespierre, announced: "Terror is nothing other than justice, prompt, severe, inflexible; it is therefore an emanation [expression] of virtue; it is not so much a special principle as it is a consequence of the general principle of democracy applied to our country's most urgent needs."

This brought to France what became known as the "Reign of Terror". By the time it was over, between 25,000 and 40,000 people had been executed by guillotine. In the end, Robespierre himself was thought to be an enemy of the revolution and executed.

> *The "Terror"*

The aftermath of the French Revolution of 1789 brought the words "terror" and "terrorism" into use.

The rise of the anarchist

In the 19th century opposition to other monarchs led to more acts of European terrorism. **Anarchists** were responsible for much of the terror. An anarchist is an individual who objects to any government rule or authority. Anarchists wanted to use direct action to end government rule, often through an individual act of terror—an assassination or bombing. The purpose of these attacks was to eliminate oppressive rulers and encourage citizens to support their cause. Anarchists claimed to want a more equal society; their targets were people who had more power and social standing, including political leaders, members of royal families, and wealthy individuals. In Russia anarchists opposed the oppressive rule of the Csar, the Russian emperor.

Russian anarchists, supported by poor peasants and landless farmers, repeatedly tried to assassinate Csar Alexander II. They succeeded on 1 March 1881. Terror had become a popular political weapon. The political use of terror was the anarchists' tool to change the social order of Europe. They believed that the assassination of the kings and queens would lead to public uprisings and popular revolts.

In 1894 an anarchist stabbed Sadi Carnot, President of France, to death. Four years later, the Empress Elizabeth of Austria was killed. From 1895 to 1925 more than a dozen European leaders were assassinated. Despite the assassination of U.S., Russian, French, Greek, Italian, and Spanish leaders, anarchists were unable to change the traditional political and social order.

 Terrorism's influence on language

assassin [**uh**-**sas**-in] noun; a killer, especially of a political leader or other public figure.
The term referred originally to the Assassins, a secret society of Shia Muslims. From the 9th to the 14th centuries, they murdered politicians and religious leaders who refused to adopt their version of Islam.

thug [thuhg] noun; somebody, especially a criminal, who is brutal and violent.
The **Thugees** were violent gangs in India during the 18th and 9th centuries. Thug is from the Hindu word, *thag*, meaning "thief" or "deceiver". The Thugees strangled members of wealthy classes across India. They were responsible for up to one million deaths.

Recent history

In the last 100 years there have been thousands of victims of terrorist violence in markets, pubs, subways, hotels, office buildings, trains and planes. Some of the violence is caused by individuals or small groups dedicated to a particular cause. A single violent act can produce catastrophic results. On 28 June 1914, Gavrilo Princip, a member of a Serbian organization demanding independence from the Austro-Hungarian Empire, assassinated Archduke Franz Ferdinand of Austria. Austria then declared war against Serbia, leading to the start of the First World War and the deaths of millions of people.

The use of political terror continues to threaten government rule. South African Prime Minister Hendrik Verwoerd, King Faisal bin Abdul Aziz Al Saud of Saudi Arabia, President Anwar Sadat of Egypt, Prime Minister Indira Gandhi of India, former Israeli Prime Minister Yitzhak Rabin, and Rosalie Gicanda, the last Tutsi queen of Rwanda, have all been assassinated in the past 40 years. Leading peace and human rights activists have also been killed. The Reverend Martin Luther King, Jr., the leader of the civil rights movement in the United States, was assassinated by a white supremacist in 1968.

Today terrorist attacks are often organized to generate fear and substantial publicity. Media reports of acts of terror help to publicize terror groups' issues. Extreme and violent behaviour can attract the world's attention. An example of this is the kidnapping and execution of Israeli athletes and coaches during the 1972 Munich Olympic Games by members of the Palestinian "Black September" organization.

State sponsors of terrorism

In addition to individual assassins and terror groups, there are also countries that sponsor terrorist acts in other countries. This is done to support revolution, disrupt public order, and for many of the same reasons as terrorist acts by individuals. The "state sponsors of terror" are responsible for bombings, kidnappings, executions, and other violent threats. The United Nations accused the Libyan government of two serious acts of terror, the bombings of a Pan Am jet over Scotland (1988) and a UTA plane in Niger (1989). These attacks caused the deaths of more than 400 innocent people.

The terror to come?

Police agencies, military officials, and counter-terrorism experts are concerned about future terrorism. Improvements in weapons technology will produce more powerful explosives. New developments will also make weapons harder to detect. Terrorists may also be able to purchase or produce weapons of mass destruction. These include biological, chemical, radiological, and nuclear weapons that can put thousands or even hundreds of thousands of individuals at risk in one attack.

> *IRA terror*

The Irish Republican Army (IRA) fought for a united Ireland free of British rule for nearly 100 years. Their tactics included bombings and assassinations. They attempted to assassinate British Prime Ministers, and succeeded in killing Lord Louis Mountbatten, the uncle by marriage of Queen Elizabeth II. After co-operating in the ending of sectarian violence in Northern Ireland, the IRA ceased to be an active terrorist organization.

> *Signing the PATRIOT Act*

Some countries have adopted security laws that increase the power of the government to wiretap, investigate, or detain citizens to prevent terrorist violence. One such law is the U.S. PATRIOT Act, being signed here by U.S. President George W. Bush in October 2001. But these laws are controversial. They may limit personal freedom, privacy, and the right to a fair trial. How far should the law go to protect citizens and residents? If governments need to limit freedoms, have the terrorists won?

Thinking And Debating Skills

Good communication skills help pupils to share their ideas, participate in important discussions, and develop self-confidence. These skills include effective public speaking, research and writing, **argument**, and **refutation**. With these tools, a pupil should be able to select the best topic, organize a speech or essay, make persuasive arguments, defend those arguments, and entertain or hold the interest of readers or listeners.

In some cases, people appear to speak with one voice about an issue. Terrorism is one of those issues. Few are willing to argue in favour of violence that may threaten to harm innocent civilians. It may seem that there is little to debate about terrorism, but that is not the case. Terrorism is controversial because it is difficult to define. It is challenging to determine who is a terrorist. It is also difficult to decide the best solution to the problem. Should governments limit the freedoms of their own citizens to fight terrorism? Should they wage war in other countries to stop it? Is it right to prevent actions by groups struggling for democracy, freedom, or human rights against oppressive governments? Which tactics should governments use to try to prevent terrorism? Should governments ever negotiate with terrorists? Terrorism is a complex subject and must be carefully examined to create good presentations that can influence the opinions and behaviour of others.

Effective communication skills

The best communicators are able to combine the elements of persuasion and argument. Persuasion is the effect that the style of presentation has on a listener. For a speaker, persuasion involves speaking clearly, with sufficient *volume*. Volume (loudness) is associated with confidence and is persuasive.

Persuasive speakers use their voices to capture the attention of an audience—they emphasize some words or phrases more than others, changing the tone. A writer does the same but uses the words on paper to create direct and powerful messages. The tone that a speaker uses lets the audience know what is particularly important and what is less so. Think of the different meanings that a speaker might have in the following sentence, based on a change in *emphasis*:

- *I* saw you.

- I *saw* you.

- I saw *you*.

To be persuasive, it is necessary to keep the audience interested as a speech develops. The key tactic is *pace*, the ability to speed up or slow down the rate of delivery. Some information may be well known to the audience. At this point, the effective speaker will speed up. If the speaker presents new, challenging, or technical information, the audience will need more time to understand it. A good communicator will slow down.

Organization

Effective speakers organize their thoughts. The best model for organization is the simple story—introduction, body, and conclusion. An *introduction* should attract the attention of the audience and prepare it to listen. This is particularly important if the topic is a controversial one, such as terrorism. An audience listening to a presentation on terrorism will already know some of the issues and have strong opinions. A good communicator will want the audience to pay attention to the information in the speech, so using **anecdotes**, quotations, surprising information or statistics, or humour can create an appealing opening. During an introduction, a speaker should also let the audience know the topic or main point of the presentation.

The *body* of the speech should set out two or three arguments to convince the listeners that the speaker is more likely to be right about the topic. The issues in the body of the speech should be well organized. These could be listed by order of importance, by cause, or in a timeline. Finally, a speaker should offer a powerful *conclusion*. A conclusion, with a dramatic or meaningful ending, should summarize the point of the speech without repeating it. If there is a single thought that a speaker would like everyone to remember about the presentation, it should be mentioned in the conclusion.

Although there are other tactics for public speaking, if a speaker has volume, emphasis, pace, and organization, it is likely that she or he can deliver a confident presentation on any subject to almost any audience.

> *Debate is used to persuade*
People need to understand that they cannot simply ignore the opinions of others, nor can they surrender to someone with powerful ideas. A person can responsibly use public speaking and debating skills to encourage others to listen, respect different points of view and, on occasion, change minds.

Presenting an argument

So what is an argument? Most people think of it as a simple disagreement. An argument certainly includes a statement of an opinion, perhaps of disagreement, but that is not all. A genuine argument adds more. An argument is the statement of an opinion that is supported by *reasoning* and *evidence*. An argument has three parts:

1. **A**ssertion

2. **R**easoning

3. **E**vidence

The parts of an argument can be remembered by the code **A – R – E**.

What is an *assertion*? An assertion is the brief statement of an opinion. It is the fact or claim that a complete argument proves. Examples of assertions include:

- The koala is the sweetest animal.

- Television entertainment has too many advertisements.

- Athletes should not be able to use performance-enhancing drugs.

- Too many people in the world do not have access to fresh water.

The second step of an argument is *reasoning*. Reasoning is the explanation of an assertion. It provides the logic, the critical thinking, the analysis of an argument. Reasoning answers the question: WHY? Why do people not have fresh water? Why should athletes not use performance-enhancing drugs?

The third and final step in making an argument is *evidence*. Evidence is factual support for your reasoning. Evidence is the factual material, general statistics, historical and contemporary examples, expert testimonies, personal and biographical stories, and other resources that support reasoning. Evidence is convincing because it involves information that provides proof for a well-reasoned idea. It is important to avoid opinions that are based on weak or suspicious evidence. (A significant number of people believe the Earth has been visited by aliens. In a survey, one in five secondary school pupils in the United States thought Germany was an ally of the U.S. during the Second World War. Twenty percent of Americans are not sure if the Earth revolves around the Sun. In a recent survey of British children aged 10–14, less than half knew that Winston Churchill was prime minister during the Second World War. Many claimed that Saddam Hussein's Iraq possessed weapons of mass destruction.) The need for evidence should encourage careful research from different sources, such as news broadcasts, books, encyclopedias, and magazines.

This is the best way to make sure that ideas are supported with the most up-to-date and accurate information.

Refuting an argument

It is not enough to have an argument. It is not enough to successfully anticipate opposing points. An effective debater must also be prepared to disprove any opposing arguments. The skill used to defeat the arguments of another person is called *refutation*. Refutation is the process of proving that a claim or argument is wrong.

An idea can be challenged in a number of ways. A debater can challenge the reasoning, showing that the argument is not well thought out or illogical. For example, someone might argue that governments need to prevent terrorism to protect democracy. He or she might say that it would be a good idea to spy on political organizations, restrict a free press that might support terrorist causes, hold terrorist suspects in jail without charge, or use torture to get information that could stop an attack. The person replying to the argument might say that the government would then be taking actions that are anti-democratic—destroying democracy in order to save it.

It is also possible to challenge the facts, the evidence. It is possible to challenge the source of facts. Some information sources are not experts; they do not have the knowledge to have a meaningful opinion on a topic. Other sources have **biases**, which prevent fair comments. Sometimes the information is not current. It is too old or events have changed. Evidence may not make sense. In the same way that one can analyze reasoning, it is possible to examine evidence to discover if an expert's story or information makes sense. A debater can also counter evidence with other expert opinions, statistics, or other proof.

 What to consider when challenging facts

✔ **Qualified source?**

✔ **Biased?**

✔ **Recent information?**

✔ **Sensible?**

✔ **Contradictory proof from other experts?**

> *Chechen and Russian violence involves acts of terror*

Chechens have resisted Russian occupation for 200 years. In the recent struggle for independence, hundreds of Russians and Chechens were killed in bombings and assassinations that led to the Russian invasion of Chechnya in 1994. More than 100,000 people, mostly Chechen civilians, have lost their lives. After so many years of violence and bitter fighting, will it be possible to negotiate peace?

How Can We Negotiate With Terrorists?

I s it possible to negotiate with terrorists? Are terrorists willing to show respect for or think carefully about someone else's feelings or position? Are the victims of terror willing to listen calmly to the point of view of their attackers?

Consider the words of people who have carried out assassinations. Could they ever have negotiated with their enemies? Leon Czolgosz, the anarchist assassin of U.S. President William McKinley in 1901, testified at his trial, "I killed the President because he was the enemy of the good people—the good working people. I done my duty. I am not sorry for my crime." Yigal Amir, the law student responsible for shooting former Israeli Prime Minister Yitzhak Rabin in 1995, was not sorry for his action. He claimed that the murder was God's will. The brother of the assassin of the non-violent campaigner for the independence of India, Mohandas Gandhi, is another person not willing to apologize for past behaviour. He was part of the conspiracy to kill Gandhi, and spent 17 years in prison for that crime. About the assassination, Gopal Godse proudly announced, "I do not regret it in the least … What we did was in the interest of the nation. Gandhi had to die because he betrayed Hindus by backing the creation of Pakistan."

Are governments willing to negotiate with terrorists?

There are a number of factors that make it difficult for police, justice, and political officials to negotiate with terrorist organizations. If a terrorist threat or action is recent, it may be too soon to communicate with an individual or group. It would be difficult, for example, with grieving families and a criminal investigation underway, for a political leader to begin negotiations with the hijackers of an aircraft. If terror threats, suicide bombings, and missile attacks are ongoing, it is particularly difficult to begin bargaining. Continued attacks undermine the trust that you need to have good discussions with an enemy about the future. Of course, some acts of terror may be too severe to imagine effective and open negotiations.

After the attacks of 11 September 2001 on the United States, with nearly 3,000 dead civilians, it would have been impossible to open channels of communication with those behind the atrocities. The 9/11 attacks caused the single greatest loss of life in an act of terror in U.S. history. In addition to local damage, the attacks affected the international economy. According to the World Bank, the economic losses from the terror assault meant that 40,000 children worldwide were more likely to die from disease and malnutrition; the decrease in economic growth could force more than 10 million into extreme poverty. The severe damage and the loss of life would continue to be a barrier to future negotiations with the organizations behind the attacks.

If a group is labelled as a "terrorist organization", governments feel less pressure to negotiate. Because there is little sympathy for terrorists, once a group has been labelled "terrorist" it loses support for its cause. This happens whether its complaints about government mistreatment or persecution are fair or not. The terrorist label also reduces the amount of international support that an organization might receive. It is less likely to get humanitarian aid or international pressure for negotiations. There is less likelihood that there will be a peaceful outcome.

Change and perseverance

It may take a considerable amount of time or a change in leadership for a terrorist organization, a government, or both, to create the conditions for negotiations. New leaders may be able to avoid the hostility of the past. They may signal future co-operation. There have been negotiations at difficult times. After years of terrorist acts and hundreds of deaths, the IRA and the British government began secret negotiations over the violence in Northern Ireland. Despite continued bombings, kidnappings, and assassinations by both sides, the Republicans and Unionists, talks continued. These discussions led to more open negotiations and peace agreements in the 1990s. After many years of bargaining, some successes, and some failed agreements, the IRA officially ended its struggle and agreed to disarm. Although there are still serious political differences to solve in Northern Ireland, negotiations and disarmament are the kinds of changes that can create possibilities for peace.

> *Government security measures can upset the public*
Governments may engage in aggressive or oppressive behaviour. This is often done to protect national security and prevent acts of terror. Nevertheless, street searches and identification checkpoints may make the people who undergo them bitter and angry. In some cases, military and police efforts to reduce terror can have the opposite effect.

How do you negotiate?

Governments and terrorist organizations may negotiate publicly, in secret, or through another group or organization. They may negotiate in an open and fair manner. They can also use negotiations to deceive the other side or delay military or terror actions. If they negotiate fairly, it is called negotiating "in **good faith**". If they lie or try to manipulate the other side, it is called negotiating "in **bad faith**".

Negotiations are only one part of a strategy to reduce terrorism. An effective government approach to terrorism may include negotiations, but must also include other policies. Negotiations will not work, for example, if a government appears to be weak. A terrorist organization has no reason to co-operate with an opposing force if it can defeat it. The government must show its strength. It can do this through military action, police surveillance and investigation, national security defences, and national and international support in the struggle against terrorism.

Military and financial responses

If terrorists participate in bombings, assassinations, and kidnappings, the armed forces can respond to the threat with direct assaults on terrorist bases and hideouts. These actions put pressure on terrorist groups and weaken their forces and resources. Aggressive military action often encourages terror groups to negotiate. A government may also use its criminal justice system against terrorist threats. It can co-ordinate national police and justice officials to investigate and prosecute terrorist crimes. The government can work with other countries and international organizations to stop the free movement of terrorists from one country to the next. Governments can work with banks to track and limit the money that supplies terrorist groups. A government can also increase its own security, protecting its transport, economic, and political centres from terrorist attacks.

The decision to choose to negotiate is often in the hands of the terrorists. Because of the secrecy of terrorist groups, it is difficult for the authorities to identify which terrorist leader they should talk to. If they do not negotiate with the right person or group, their efforts will not pay off. For this reason, negotiations usually need the terrorist organization to make the first move.

Fear and surprise are the prime allies of the terrorist. The public is terrified by unexpected assaults on innocent people, particularly in public places that are difficult to avoid. The government, which is interested in protecting its citizens, must reply to public fear. If terrorist actions are successful, terrorist leaders are in a position of strength and seem powerful. That gives governments a reason to act or negotiate. For this reason, successful government responses almost always require authorities to use military or police action and national security defences to reduce the power of terrorist organizations.

> *Truck bombing of the Murrah Federal Building in Oklahoma City*
Negotiation is not possible in the case of a surprise attack. On 9 April 1995, a truck bomb destroyed the U.S. government office building in Oklahoma City. Until 9/11, it was the deadliest domestic terrorist attack in the United States. One hundred and sixty-eight people, including young children at a government nursery, were killed and hundreds were injured. Two men with links to secretive, anti-government organizations, usually known as "militias", carried out the bombing. Both were "home grown" terrorists: white, American-born, and claiming to have acted independently. Bomber Timothy McVeigh was executed in 2001 for his part in the attack.

Skill and tactics

There are tactics that effective negotiators use to make sure they will succeed. First, they try to understand the issue from the point of view of their opponent. This is the skill of *argument anticipation.* Negotiators do not want to be taken by surprise. They want to be prepared for the best arguments from their opponents. Secondly, effective negotiators have *clearly defined goals.* They need to understand what they want; they need to know how the other side can help them reach their goals. Thirdly, they work on the *easy issues first.* This encourages the two sides to have some bargaining successes, which increases trust and makes later breakthroughs more likely. Fourthly, they **compromise**. A compromise is an agreement to accept less than everything you want.

People have to negotiate because they cannot otherwise settle their differences. Those differences still separate the groups. That means that each side will have to be more accepting of the position of the other side to reach a final settlement. To do that, they will have to take a bit less than they wanted. If both sides do this, the negotiated agreement will still seem fair to all.

> *Government negotiations for hostage and prisoner release*
> Governments negotiate with terrorist organizations for a variety of reasons. These include the release of hostages, prisoner exchanges, ceasefire agreements, disarmament plans, and peacekeeping efforts. Successful efforts can lead to additional and more meaningful negotiations.

Terrorist violence and negotiation 2000–2006

Negotiations may reduce the amount of violence, even if hostilities continue. For example, the Colombian government has started a peace process with the second-largest rebel group, the National Liberation Army, and peace negotiations have begun between the government in Uganda and the Lord's Resistance Army. In these cases, negotiations have reduced the incidents of terrorist violence. This table shows a relationship between terrorist violence, negotiation, and the number of fatalities. Does negotiation help?

Country	Terrorist fatalities	Is violence increasing?	Are negotiations taking place?
Iraq	11,611	Yes	No
United States	2,990	No	Yes
Colombia	1,177	No	Yes
Russia	945	Yes	No
India	899	Yes	No
Pakistan	855	Yes	No
Afghanistan	790	Yes	No
Israel	728	No	Yes
West Bank	486	Yes	No
Philippines	485	No	Yes
Indonesia	465	No	Yes
Uganda	450	No	Yes
Thailand	305	Yes	No
Angola	257	No	Yes
Sri Lanka	251	No	Yes

[Terrorist Incidents, 2000 – 2006, as reported by the Memorial Institute for the Prevention of Terrorism Knowledge Base]

Methods of negotiation

There are different methods of negotiation that can be used by governments and terrorist organizations. These are based on the strength of the government and the terrorist opposition, the issue they are negotiating about, and the willingness of the government and terrorists to decrease future military action and terrorist incidents. No government or terrorist group is likely to co-operate with the other if it believes that doing so will encourage new violence.

Options for negotiation

Negotiations in good faith

✔ public negotiations

✔ secret negotiations

✔ third party negotiations

Negotiations in bad faith

✔ negotiations as a delaying tactic

✔ negotiate an agreement, but publicly attack at a later time

✔ negotiate an agreement, but privately attack at a later time

Each of the above methods has been used and each has its advantages and disadvantages. "Good faith" negotiations are the ones that groups use to get a lasting agreement. A public negotiation has the advantage of showing that those involved are trying to work with the other side to solve their problems. It encourages trust. It has the disadvantage of making either the government or the terrorist organization appear weak to its supporters, particularly to those that do not want to negotiate. Secret negotiations can eliminate some of these problems but they raise new issues. Can the negotiations be kept secret? If they are secret, won't the police investigations and terrorist assaults continue, hurting the negotiation process? **Third party negotiations**, getting another group involved in the negotiations, can be helpful. The third party cannot speak for the government or terrorist group, however, and this method can be slow.

"Bad faith" negotiations are simply phony or false ones. They almost always lead to more violence in the immediate future. They are used to delay a reaction from the other side in order to buy time to increase the people or resources for a military or political advantage.

> *World Trade Center attacks – 11 September 2001*

Some terrorist incidents are so serious that government officials are unwilling to negotiate. When hijacked planes crashed into the World Trade Center towers in New York City, this atrocity shocked people around the world. The assault killed and injured thousands of people and led to economic losses of billions of dollars. In the years since the attacks, many government leaders have been unwilling to negotiate with terrorists who might be connected with Osama bin Laden or members of his al-Qaeda network, who were responsible for the 9/11 terror plot.

Which method works best?

Here are some examples of how various negotiation methods have been used. Which do you think has the best hope of both reducing terrorism and producing long-lasting peace? Even small agreements can produce trust that can lead to future successful negotiations.

Public negotiation: Nepal

The Communist Party (Maoist) of Nepal used armed conflict in its attempt to overthrow the monarchy. More than 13,000 people died in the violence, and hundreds of thousands were forced from their homes. The government and the rebels reached a peace agreement in November 2006, which called for disarmament, elections, and a new constitution. Some groups still fear they will be excluded from the new government. Economic strikes have been called by Maoist leaders.

Secret negotiation: the Jill Carroll hostage crisis

Jill Carroll was a journalist working in Iraq. The "Revenge Brigades" kidnapped her in Baghdad. This terrorist group demanded the release of eight Iraqi women who were held by the U.S.-led coalition forces. Although there was no public negotiation, two days later six of the jailed women were freed, and Jill Carroll was released by her captors.

Third party negotiation: the Good Friday Agreement

For many years, the Irish Republican Army (IRA) had both secret and public negotiations with the British government to end the sectarian violence between Catholics and Protestants in Northern Ireland. These agreements were soon broken. In 1998 the Good Friday Agreement established a peace process. It called for prisoner releases, disarmament, and democratic power sharing. It was negotiated and reviewed by an American, former U.S. Senator George Mitchell. This took some pressure off the British government and IRA negotiators, who had fought each other fiercely.

Negotiate to delay and prepare response: Moscow theatre siege

In 2002, 42 Chechen rebels stormed the Palace of Culture in Moscow, taking 850 hostages in the theatre. Russian officials began negotiations with the terrorists. These led to the release of Muslim women and children and a man with a heart condition. The Russians used the negotiation time to surround the building with military special forces. Russian troops delivered knockout gas through the building's air conditioning system and attacked the rebels, killing all of them. But the ending of the siege cannot be called real success. One hundred and twenty-nine hostages also died in the assault, all but one from the effects of the gas.

> *No chance to negotiate in Bali*

In 2002, in a deadly act of terrorism in Indonesia, suicide and car bombings in Bali claimed the lives of 202 people, including 88 Australian tourists. More than 200 people were injured. A previously unknown extremist Islamic group was responsible for the violence. Since the first bombing, and the arrest and conviction of some of those responsible, there have been more terrorist incidents in Bali. Here people are laying flowers at the Indonesia Memorial on the third anniversary of the bombing.

> *Government terror*

Not all acts of terror are by dissenting groups against a government. Some governments commit horrible crimes against their own and other people. They may use military and police forces to commit terror or sponsor terrorist organizations in another country. The Indonesian armed forces were extraordinarily violent in East Timor—hundreds of thousands of people died. These Australian peacekeeping troops were sent to stop the bloodshed.

Government–to–Government Negotiations

Governments can be responsible for acts of terror. They can victimize their own populations through kidnapping, torture, and assassination. This may help to keep an unpopular government in power. Governments may use domestic terrorist organizations, such as paramilitary groups, to threaten or eliminate their political opponents. Paramilitary groups, which work closely with national military and police forces, are often able to use terrorist tactics under the protection of the law. Police forces and government-supported death squads have targeted union and religious leaders, street children, journalists, and opposition political parties.

Governments may also sponsor terrorist organizations in other countries. They may permit terrorist groups to establish offices from which they can raise money and plan their operations. They may provide terror organizations with intelligence to find their targets. They can provide a safe haven for terrorists trying to escape from the police. Countries can provide bases, resources, and military experts to train terrorists. Afghanistan, for example, was the training ground for al-Qaeda. State sponsors of terrorism may also fund and arm groups to carry out attacks. Various governments have been held responsible for this behaviour. The United Nations has condemned government-supported terror. State sponsors of terror have been punished by other countries, who have cut off trade and aid deals with them.

Terrorism and the United Nations

The United Nations has encouraged its member countries to work against international terrorism by co-operating in international criminal investigations, strengthening domestic laws against terrorism, and joining UN treaties designed to stop nuclear terrorism. After the 9/11 attacks on the United States, the United Nations gave legal assistance to countries to help pass new laws to prevent domestic acts of terror. Seventeen countries and international organizations adopted measures to combat terrorism. The United Nations is also involved in negotiating the end of civil wars and domestic conflicts that produce terrorist and state violence. United Nations officials are part of peace negotiations in many countries, including Lebanon and East Timor.

 United Nations opposition

The United Nations opposes terrorism by individuals, groups, or countries. In its December 1994 *Declaration on Measures to Eliminate International Terrorism,* the organization's members claimed:

> *... States Members of the United Nations solemnly reaffirm their unequivocal condemnation of all acts, methods, and practices of terrorism as criminal and unjustifiable, wherever and by whomsoever committed, including those which jeopardize the friendly relations among States and peoples and threaten the territorial integrity and security of States.*

Many countries and international organizations want to negotiate to reduce the threat of state-sponsored terrorism. Their major concern is to limit the spread of weapons of mass destruction. These weapons permit a person or small group to threaten a large population. A government has the resources, laboratories, and skilled workers to produce these very destructive weapons. Government-sponsored mass destruction might include biological agents, such as a virus, that could destroy a food supply. Governments might have the materials to build a nuclear weapon or radiological weapon, such as a "dirty bomb" of plutonium that could contaminate an area of a city.

State-sponsored terrorism could use weapons that might kill and injure many tens of thousands of people or threaten a nation's economy. This makes these weapons especially valuable for terrorist organizations.

> *Libya was responsible for the Lockerbie bombing*
Abdelbaset Ali Mohmed Al Megrahi, a former Libyan
intelligence officer, was convicted of the bombing of Pan
American flight 103. The plane exploded over Lockerbie,
Scotland in 1988, killing 270 people. The Libyan
government and its president, Colonel Gaddafi, shown here
in 2003 with British Prime Minister Tony Blair, denied any
connection with the bombing for years, but finally admitted
Libya's responsibility to the United Nations.

Many countries have the knowledge and resources to produce weapons of
mass destruction. Some countries have the ability to make even more powerful
explosives. Two countries that have been accused of sponsoring terrorism have,
or may develop, nuclear weapons. North Korea has already tested one nuclear
bomb; Iran may develop one. Unless these and other countries are encouraged
to co-operate with international organizations, or kept in check in other ways,
they might be willing to sell or trade advanced weapons to terrorists.

The United Nations and others are negotiating with Iran to restrict nuclear
weapons. The six-party talks, involving North Korea, South Korea, China, Russia,
Japan, and the United States aim to eliminate the further development of a
nuclear threat. If the negotiations are successful, the talks might produce other
efforts to limit state support of terrorist organizations.

The West and Islam

Terrorist conflict may increase because of rising tension between Western countries and those with a substantial Muslim population. There have certainly been significant positive influences and efforts for co-operation between political and social Western and Islamic groups. And Islam, like other major world religions, does not offer support for violence, particularly acts of terror against the innocent. But some of the important modern values of the West—such as democracy and individualism—may be at odds with core values of some aspects of traditional Muslim cultural life, which emphasize belief and community. This can produce differences of opinion, ignorance, and stereotyping, which make miscommunication and conflict more likely.

Some conflict may occur because of the interdependence between Islamic countries and the West. The Muslim states of the Middle East are major oil producers. Countries in the West need the oil, and the supplying countries want the money from oil sales. Other Muslim countries, such as Indonesia, Pakistan, and Egypt, are important regional powers and major trading partners for the West. Countries of the world must be on good terms with Islamic countries that already have nuclear weapons, such as Pakistan, or may get them in the future, such as Iran.

Radical groups

Many Islamic countries have religious and political groups that participate in or support terror. These terrorist organizations are usually connected with extreme or radical versions of Islam. These groups are a very small minority of the population in Islamic countries but they may have strong support in one or more regions, which makes it hard to investigate or remove them. The groups may oppose both the West and their own governments, which the terror groups often label as corrupt and impure. The Taliban of Afghanistan may be the most extreme example. The Taliban practise a radical, fundamentalist form of Islam. Although the majority of Afghan citizens did not belong to or support the Taliban, they were unable to stop the Taliban when they came to power by force. The Taliban banned the education of women and refused them the right to vote or drive. They did not permit television—they even had public executions of television sets. Although few Muslims would agree with these practices, it does not take a large number of terrorists to achieve significant control through violence.

Currently a list of countries with substantial Muslim populations is also a list of countries with a significant number of terrorist organizations: Afghanistan, Pakistan, Indonesia, Iran, Iraq, Syria, Sudan, Egypt, Bangladesh, Philippines, and Thailand. In just the first few months of 2007, for example, various terrorists connected to radical Islamic organizations shelled the Bagram Air Base in

Afghanistan, caused bombings in shopping areas in Bangkok, Thailand and Casablanca, Morocco, attacked a train travelling from India to Pakistan, bombed buses in Sri Lanka and office buildings in Turkey, and sponsored suicide and car bombings in Iran, Iraq, and Lebanon. Other governments must carefully negotiate their relationships with these countries in order to reduce the threat of domestic and international terrorist reactions. They can use a variety of positive steps to seek co-operation with these important Muslim countries and lessen the influence of terrorist groups. These efforts include diplomacy, foreign and humanitarian assistance, educational and business exchanges, and military support. If these do not work, they might try negative policies, such as economic and travel restrictions, to force them to increase their domestic anti-terrorist policies.

> *Terrorism grows in places without functioning governments*
Somalia is a country without a working central government. Large areas are entirely lawless with warlords in control. This makes it easy for terrorists to hide, train, and plan operations. There is support for al-Qaeda and other Islamic terrorist groups among Somalia's Muslim villages.

States that sponsor terrorism

Members of the United Nations, government leaders, and human rights organizations have accused some powerful and influential countries of sponsoring state terror. The United Kingdom, United States, and Australia identified Libya, Iran, and Syria as governments that sponsor terrorism. The United Nations passed resolutions against Iran and Sudan.

Iran

Iran provides funding, weapons, and training, to numerous terrorist groups, including Hamas, Palestinian Islamic Jihad, and Hezbollah. Hamas and Palestinian Islamic Jihad support the destruction of Israel. These organizations have conducted a number of terrorist operations in Israel. Palestinian Islamic Jihad also opposes what it describes as "corrupt Arab governments" and seeks to overthrow the Egyptian government. Iran established Hezbollah with Lebanese Muslims in the 1980s. Hezbollah was responsible for the bombing of the barracks of U.S. Marines in Beirut, Lebanon in 1983, killing 241 soldiers. Argentine police officials also hold the organization responsible for the bombing of the Israeli Embassy in Buenos Aires in 1992.

Pakistan

Pakistan has been accused of supporting Taliban training camps along the Afghanistan border. The country is also accused of harbouring terrorists, including Osama bin Laden and the former Taliban leader of Afghanistan, Mullah Omar. Pakistan supports rebel groups trying to overthrow Indian control of Kashmir, in a disputed region that borders Pakistan and India. The United Nations has asked Pakistan to reduce its support for groups within its territory. The Khan network, an international nuclear weapons smuggling operation, was centred in Pakistan. It sent equipment used in making nuclear weapons to Libya, Iran, and North Korea.

Sudan

Sudan has been a safe haven for a number of terrorist organizations, including al-Qaeda, Egyptian Islamic Jihad, Palestinian Islamic Jihad, Hamas, and Hezbollah. Although these groups have not conducted operations in Sudan, they have planned and trained for terrorist missions in other countries. The attempt to assassinate Egyptian President Hosni Mubarak in Ethiopia was planned by Egyptian Islamic Jihad in Sudan. The United Nations placed economic penalties on Sudan for refusing to turn over the people involved in the plot. Al-Qaeda bombings of the U.S. embassies in Tanzania and Kenya were also planned in Sudan. The attacks killed 224 people. The Sudanese government is also accused of supporting the Janjaweed paramilitary Arab groups. The Janjaweed is responsible for massacres, rapes, and human rights violation in the non-Muslim Darfur region of Sudan. More than 200,000 people have been killed there, and more than 2 million have been driven from their homes.

Syria

Although it has not been directly involved in terrorist activities for 20 years, Syria supports terrorist groups that operate within its borders. It provides weapons, training, and financial support for Hezbollah in Lebanon. Hezbollah has attacked Israel and engages in armed struggle with Lebanese security forces. Other organizations that participate in terrorist acts, including Hamas and Palestinian Islamic Jihad, have their offices in Damascus, Syria. These groups have also sponsored suicide bombings and missile attacks on Israel. In February 2005, the United Nations investigation into the assassination of a former Lebanese Prime Minister reported that Syrian intelligence officials may have been involved. But Syria has also worked against some extremist groups, arresting Islamic militants in its country, closing its border with Iraq to insurgents and terrorists, and co-operating with some U.S. counter-terrorism operations.

Your enemy's enemy

Some countries that are better known for fighting against terrorism have also had relationships with terror groups. This often occurs when the terror organization may be helpful in a conflict with another country or more dangerous terrorist threat. The United States may be an example of this. In late 1979, the Soviet Union invaded Afghanistan. Throughout the 1980s the United States tried to help the people of Afghanistan resist the Soviet military forces. The U.S. supported the **mujahideen**, the name given to the various groups of Muslim rebels who fought against the Soviets. The U.S. government made the decision that these local rebels would be able to effectively fight against the Soviets. They did fight for years and finally forced the Soviet troops from the country. Some of the money and arms the United States supplied probably found its way to groups within the *mujahideen*, such as the Taliban and al-Qaeda. These organizations later became terrorist enemies of the United States and others.

Lebanon—caught in the middle

Lebanon has become the country where much fighting in the Middle East conflict takes place. This is partially due to its geographic location. The other reason is the large number of Palestinian refugee camps (approximately 13) which have become home to militants armed by other countries.

A response to Iraq?

In 2003 military forces from more than 20 countries entered Iraq to overthrow Saddam Hussein. Those countries, including the United States, United Kingdom, and Spain, argued that it would be better to stop terror in Iraq rather than wait until it reached their own countries. However, after the war in Iraq started, bombings in Madrid (2004) and London (2005) killed 243 people and injured nearly 3,000. Many think that because Spain and the United Kingdom sent troops to Iraq, terrorists responded by attacking them at home. This is why leaders have to take great care when they make a decision about what to do to combat terrorism. They have to try to make sure that their decision is a good one for the present and for the future. A careful decision-maker, or a debater, must think about the consequences of an action. Will a decision backfire? It is a good idea to consider blowback (see below) and other possible results of actions.

> *Negotiations can be stopped by new acts of violence*
> The Revolutionary Armed Forces of Colombia (FARC) are a rebel group that has participated in bombings, kidnappings, and attacks on government officials. At a meeting, shown above, FARC and the government agreed to peace negotiations. As preparations for negotiations began, two bombings and an attack on a police station led to the government calling off the talks.

 Blowback

"Blowback" is a U.S. CIA (Central Intelligence Agency) term. It refers to taking an action that a country believes will work in its favour, but in the long run turns out to work against it.

> *Peace negotiations do not necessarily lead to peace*
The Liberation Tigers of Tamil ("Tamil Tigers") have fought a bloody territorial conflict with the government of Sri Lanka. Nearly 75,000 people have died from terrorist and military violence, but negotiations have not stopped the violence.

Why is government-to-government negotiation more successful?

It is easier for governments to negotiate with each other than it is for governments to negotiate with terrorist organizations. There are three main reasons for this:

- Governments have an established leader. It is possible to identify the leader of a government. To avoid capture and to protect friends and family, a leader of a terrorist organization will usually hide his or her identity.
- There are established organizations for negotiation. The United Nations and regional organizations, such as the European Union and the African Union, are available for countries to bring complaints to and help solve problems. International organizations may be able to support a peace agreement by sending peacekeeping troops.
- There are shared allies or neutral countries to help negotiate. It is possible that another country may be an ally of both the countries that are involved in a dispute. With the six-party talks, China was able to work with both North Korea and the United States to get the discussions started.

> *Osama bin Laden is the world's most wanted terrorist*
Osama bin Laden is the most wanted terrorist in the world.
Among other acts of terror, his al-Qaeda organization was
responsible for organizing the 9/11 attacks on the United
States. In 2007 the U.S. government raised the reward for
information leading to his arrest to U.S.$50 million.

Would You Negotiate?

Have you ever had to sit down and work out a serious disagreement with another person? It can be intellectually challenging and emotionally exhausting. Could you imagine having a discussion with an enemy, one who may have threatened you or your family, or a person responsible for an act of terror that took hundreds of innocent lives in your community? Opening negotiations with a dangerous and violent opponent is one of the most difficult decisions that a leader can make. Could you do it? Could you trust an enemy enough to begin the process to make peace? Could you make the political decision to negotiate?

Each year many countries and groups are responsible for thousands of acts of terror. The terrorists have included Libyan military intelligence officers, farmer-soldiers in Angola, drug dealers in Colombia, white supremacists in Germany, Peruvian rural peasant groups, assassins of journalists in Russia, Muslim extremists in the Philippines, Catholics and Protestants in Northern Ireland, Kurdish and Tamil nationalists, and Japanese cult followers. Some have genuine grievances. They represent people who are victims of oppression, persecution, human rights violations, torture, and extreme violence. Others may have radical, unfair, or bizarre demands. One potential solution to violence involves negotiation—a discussion with the goal of settling differences. Can negotiating with terrorists ever work?

Thinking the unthinkable

It may seem impossible for the United States to negotiate with Iraqi insurgents. President George W. Bush has labelled the struggle in Iraq as the frontline in the war on terror. Insurgents in Iraq have been responsible for the deaths of thousands of American soldiers. Throughout history, however, events happen that could not have been imagined by most people, such as Irish Republican Army disarmament, a black leader of the Republic of South Africa, or the collapse of the Soviet Union. In the 1980s, it was impossible for Britain and the United States to negotiate with their then greatest terrorist threat—Muammar Gaddafi, Libya's leader. In the past few years, both countries have negotiated with Gaddafi. In fact, the U.S. military, State Department, and CIA have held some talks with Iraqi insurgent leaders to try to reduce foreign fighters in Iraq, stop the violence, get Iraqis to co-operate with their new government, and reduce the influence of Iran. Is this a good idea? Does it encourage the terrorists or help reduce the violence in that country?

What do you think?

1. Should the United States negotiate with Iraqi insurgents? Should the United States negotiate with insurgents responsible for attacks on Americans?
2. Which negotiation strategy would you choose and why? Public negotiation? Secret negotiation? Third-party negotiation? Negotiate and attack anyway?
3. What would you negotiate for? What would you try to get the insurgents to agree to do?
4. What would you be willing to agree to in order to get their co-operation? How would you compromise?
5. What do you think the public reaction would be to any negotiation with Iraqis who had previously attacked troops? Do you think you could get the American public to support negotiations? How would you do it?

Talks with radicals called key to ending violence:
U.S. must negotiate with insurgents and militias, experts say

As President Bush prepares this week to announce a new plan for the war in Iraq, doubts are growing in Baghdad and among some international analysts over whether U.S. attempts to reconcile Iraq's warring factions are excluding the very people who need reconciling—the Sunni-led insurgents and their archenemies, the Shiite militias. Put simply, the question is this: With more than 3,000 American troops and many tens of thousands of Iraqis killed since the U.S.-led invasion in 2003, is it time to speak to the killers themselves? … "The U.S. administration's problem is that it has been negotiating with (Iraqi) politicians and parties that have no public support, so they are unable to help the United States withdraw from Iraq," said a former brigadier general in Saddam Hussein's army who said he is "close" to the Sunni-led insurgency and asked that his name be withheld for security reasons.

In *Chronicle* interviews, the former army general and a former division general of the Republican Guard, the elite branch of Hussein's military, said leading factions of the insurgency are willing to engage in negotiations through the United Nations … Both men said that leaders of several insurgent organizations—Mujahideen Army, Muhammad's Army, Iraqi Islamic Army, General Command for Armed Forces, 20th Revolution Brigades and "some groups" from Ansar al-Sunnah Army, but excluding al Qaeda—met early last year and agreed on a common negotiating position that would be led by Izzat Ibrahim, Hussein's former second-in-command … Mudafar al-Amin, who was Iraq's ambassador to Britain from 1999 until the U.S.-led invasion in March 2003, said most insurgent leaders are willing to negotiate. "Look at the Lebanese civil war, look at Angola. They each fought for 20 years, and finally they had to talk and find a reasonable solution to take their countries out of the ruins," said al-Amin, who lives in Jordan. "The situation now is to nobody's benefit. The country has been made into hell."

[Robert Collier, *San Francisco Chronicle* Staff Writer, Sunday 7 January 2007 http://www.sfgate.com/cgi-bin/article.cgi?f=/c/a/2007/01/07/MNG1FNEEHB1.DTL]

> *Hidden enemies*
This destruction in the Iraqi city of Kirkuk was caused by a suicide car bomber.

Success and failure

Negotiations may not work as planned. In the 1970s, the British government opened secret negotiations with the Irish Republican Army. These discussions continued, despite numerous bombings, assassinations, and arrests. Eventually, negotiators were able to reach out to Unionist leaders, IRA supporters, and political parties in Northern Ireland, as well as the British and Irish governments. The process of negotiation has taken more than 30 years, but more formal agreements are now in place.

Problems can arise even from successful negotiations. In 2003 Muammar Gaddafi, the Libyan leader, accepted responsibility for the Libyan role in the explosion and crash of a plane over Lockerbie, Scotland in 1988. Gaddafi agreed to surrender his weapons of mass destruction. He also agreed to pay U.S.$2.7 billion to the families of the victims of the bombing. Negotiations ended and the British announced a deal. Gaddafi later demanded a change in the agreement. He has asked to pay a reduced amount to families, and wants the release of the Libyan convicted for planting the bomb on the plane. There is no final settlement.

> *Is it reasonable to negotiate with a democratically elected terrorist organization?*
Hamas is a Palestinian organization that was elected to majority control of the Palestinian National Authority in 2006. It opposes the existence of Israel, and calls for an Islamist state to replace it. It conducts military operations against Israel, including suicide bombings. The United Kingdom, Australia, Canada, the European Union, and the United States consider Hamas to be a terrorist organization.

Would you negotiate with these people?

Person A

- He led the **Irgun**, a terrorist organization. Israel's first prime minister, David Ben-Gurion, criticized the group as "an enemy of the Jewish people".

- He issued death warrants for British soldiers in Palestine.

- In 1948, he planned and ordered the destruction of the King David Hotel in Jerusalem. The hotel was the centre of British military operations in Palestine. The bombing was the deadliest terrorist attack in the British Palestinian Mandate. Ninety-one people, including 40 Arab and Jewish civilians, were killed in the attack.

- He directed the attack on the Deir Yassin village. More than 100 Arab civilians, mostly women, children, and the elderly, were killed. The village attack was part of a campaign to drive Arab settlers from areas around Jerusalem. Tens of thousands of people fled after the village was destroyed.

Person B

- He was the leader of the military wing of the banned organization, "Spear of the Nation". The organization carried out guerilla warfare in urban areas and other acts of terror for nearly 30 years.

- He organized bombing operations against civilian, military, and government targets. A single car bombing of a pub killed and wounded 75 people.

- His organization provided paramilitary training for rebel and terrorist groups in southern Africa throughout the 1960s and 1970s. The terrorists who received training participated in armed conflict in Angola and Mozambique.

- He was jailed for 27 years for treason. During that time, he would not reject armed struggle.

And they are...

Person A: Menachem Begin

- He defended Jewish settlers in Palestine against violence.
- He became the democratically elected Prime Minister of Israel.
- He negotiated the Camp David Accords in 1978 with U.S. President Jimmy Carter and Egyptian President Anwar Sadat, a peace agreement that removed Israeli Defence Forces from the Sinai Peninsula and returned the land to Egypt. This became the basis of later negotiations between Israel and the Palestinian Liberation Organization and the Kingdom of Jordan.

> *Menachem Begin (1913–1992)*

- In 1979, he established a lasting peace treaty between Egypt and Israel, the first such agreement between an Arab country and Israel. The treaty has kept the peace for nearly 30 years.
- He was awarded the 1978 Nobel Peace Prize.

Person B: Nelson Mandela

- He resisted apartheid, racial separation and discrimination in his native country of South Africa. Apartheid was the forcible legal separation of people by race. The black majority of citizens were excluded from the rights and legal protections of the government. Africans and other non-white residents of South Africa were denied the right to vote. They did not have equal housing, education, medical care, or employment opportunities.
- He participated in opposition against the government that was non-violent until the police and military massacred protestors.

> *Nelson Mandela (1918–)*

- He was the first president of South Africa elected by a democratic vote that included all its citizens.
- He has received more than 100 national and international human rights awards and other honours. He won the Nobel Peace prize in 1993.

Did the information on this page challenge the opinions you developed after reading page 49?

Organizing a debate or discussion

Debate and serious discussion are exercises in critical thinking. The participants carefully test ideas—offering proof and challenging the arguments of opponents. A complex subject, such as whether it is possible to negotiate with terrorists, presents many challenges, but the value of debate and discussion is that they do not produce just any opinion on a topic—the process gets at the best possible defensible opinions. Each format has a particular set of rules. You can change the rules for the number of participants or the amount of time available. For any format, it is possible to add question and comment time during, in between, or after the speeches. It is also possible for an individual or group to judge a debate, voting on the outcome. For larger discussions, it is possible to ask the audience to vote on which person or team did the best job.

Debate

Two teams take part in a debate. One side (the proposition) makes a case for the topic. The other side (the opposition) argues against the case. The teams alternate speakers. The proposition team, who support the topic, speaks first and last. The first opposition speaker refutes the case. Second speakers continue with their team's points and refute new points from the other side. The final speeches are summaries of a team's best arguments.

 Speakers in a debate

✔ First speaker, proposition—5 minutes
✔ First speaker, opposition—5 minutes
✔ Second speaker, proposition—5 minutes
✔ Second speaker, opposition—5 minutes
✔ Third speaker, opposition—3 minutes
✔ Third speaker, proposition—3 minutes

Discussion

Pupils can participate as a group in a discussion on an issue. This can be a small group, four or five, or an entire class or community audience. Pupils speak for themselves and may agree or disagree with the opinions of others. An overall time limit will need to be set.

After you have done the research and participated in a discussion or debate on terrorism, what do you think about it? Have your opinions changed? Should we ever negotiate with terrorists?

Find Out More

Books

The War on Terror–Is the World a Safer Place? Gary E. Barr (Heinemann Library, 2007)

September 11, 2001, Brendan January (Heinemann Library, 2003)

Terrorism: The Impact on Our Lives, Alex Woolf (Heinemann Library, 2004)

Stormbreaker, Anthony Horowitz (Puffin Books, 2006)

Al-Qaeda: The True Story of Radical Islam, Jason Burke (Penguin Books, 2004)

Beslan, The Tragedy of School No.1, Timothy Phillips (Granta Books, 2007)

Websites

Radical Islam
http://www.bbc.co.uk/history/recent/sept_11/
This BBC website looks at the background to September 11, including the relationship between the West and the Islamic world.

Northern Ireland
http://www.bbc.co.uk/history/recent/troubles/
This BBC website does the same for the troubles in Northern Ireland.

Kaufman's Web Resources on Conflict
http://urban.csuohio.edu/~sanda/conflict.htm
Website with multiple links to negotiation and conflict management websites.

About.com: Terrorism Issues
http://terrorism.about.com/od/glossaryofterrorismterms/Glossary_of_Terrorism_Terms.htm
Hundreds of files on terrorism definitions, history, organizations, and events.

Alternative Resources on the War on Terror
http://www.pitt.edu/~ttwiss/irtf/Alternative.html
International Responsibilities Task Force of the American Library Association. Comprehensive list of website links and other resources featuring alternative approaches to terror analysis and prevention.

International Security and Terrorism Research
http://www.terrorism-research.com/
Comprehensive information on terrorism, including glossary and encyclopedia references to the history, organizations, and future of terrorism.

United Nations Terrorism Resources
http://www.un.org/Depts/dhl/resources/terrorism/
United Nations library resources on terrorism.

ThinkQuest – Guide to Terrorism (Oracle Education Library)
http://library.thinkquest.org/CR0212088/terhome.htm
An outstanding student-research comprehensive site on global terrorism.

Documentary films

Children of Beslan (2005)
Reflections on the 2004 Beslan massacre involving Chechen terrorists and Russian military forces.

Omagh (2004)
IRA bombing in a market square in Northern Ireland.

One Day In September (1999)
An account of the Palestinian terrorist attack during the 1972 Munich Olympics.

Glossary

anarchist someone who believes that all government and ruling classes should be abolished or destroyed

anecdote recounted story of an amusing or interesting event

argument statement designed to prove a point. It includes assertion, reasoning, and evidence (A – R – E).

assassins originally known as the Hashhashin, they were an Islamic religious society from northern Iran. They targeted Muslim rulers who had persecuted them, killing their targets in public places, not caring if they were caught. The word became assassin and a single killer is still known by that name.

bad faith negotiations unfair, manipulative, or deceitful negotiations. These are used by individuals and groups who are not interested in genuine co-operation.

bias prejudice or influence; an inclination towards a particular point of view

compromise settlement of a disagreement or dispute in which the sides agree to take less than they originally wanted

dissent practice of disagreeing with the government or other authorities. In some countries, dissent is outlawed and dissenters can be silenced, arrested, and even tortured or killed.

good faith negotiations when the sides of a negotiation trust each other and act in a fair and honest way, they are bargaining in good faith

Hamas Palestinian organization responsible for suicide bombings and other attacks in Israel. Hamas is dedicated to the creation of an independent Islamic state, as well as the elimination of Israel. In 2006, members of Hamas were elected to leadership of the Palestinian National Authority parliament.

Hezbollah Shi'ite (a form of Islam) organization in Lebanon, which is supported financially and militarily by Iran. Hezbollah is interested in establishing an Islamic government in Lebanon. It has been involved in armed struggle with security forces in Lebanon and the Israeli army. In addition to military forces,

Hezbollah officials have been elected to the Lebanese government. The organization also sponsors the construction of schools and hospitals for Palestinian refugees living in Lebanon, which makes it popular.

Irgun Jewish organization of the 1930s and 1940s that was committed to forcing the British from Palestine. They particularly wanted to end British rule because of the limits that the British placed on Jewish immigration into Palestine.

monarchy political system in which the government is ruled by a monarch, a king or queen, who rules for life

mujahideen Islamic fighters in Kashmir, Afghanistan, Iraq, and Somalia, among other places, are called this

negotiation way of influencing the decision of other people through communication and compromise

paramilitary civilian organization that is trained to fight like the police or military forces

refutation reply to an argument. It may be based on disagreement over the facts or reasoning. It can also include the presentation of new material that disproves an opposing point.

third-party negotiations negotiations that receive assistance from another person, organization, or government. If there is a dispute between two sides (parties), it may be helpful for a third party to enter the negotiation to increase the chances of success.

Thugees religious cult in India that participated in the killing of wealthy travellers. The word thug, which means brutal or violent person, comes from their name.

weapons of mass destruction weapons that can kill or injure hundreds of thousands of people. They include biological weapons (e.g., anthrax or smallpox), chemical weapons (e.g., mustard and sarin gas), radiological weapons (explosives that include radioactive elements, such as 'dirty bombs'), and nuclear weapons.

Index